new Dad Handbook

Tips, tools & tricks for new Fathers

Robert Richter

Legal blah-blah

None of the advice, tips, tools or tricks in this book are foolproof. Most were achieved by observation, trial and error. Many came from pediatricians, social workers and other experienced parents.

The best advice is, keep watching and listening.
And keep your sense of humor.

Good luck, Dad.

ISBN-10: 1495307069
ISBN-13: 978-1495307065

Dedication

To my six children and 16 foster children.

From whom I learned these tips, tools and tricks. And to whom I apologize for my many mistakes along the way.

I love you.

contents

Acknowledgements

To Dr. Padma Talcherkar, Pediatrician and lover of children.
Thank you for your generous contribution to the editing of this book
and sharing your experience with children.

And to the Children's Home + Aid Society of Illinois and their wonderful
staff of social workers and miracle workers for children and their families.
I'm grateful for my experience as a foster father and for my opportunity to
serve as Board Emeritus Trustee.

Forward

By Dr. Padma Talcherkar M.D. Pediatrician

"New Dad Handbook is especially valuable, stressing a father's need to be equally involved with the mother in raising his child. It's a practical how-to, hands-on book for new fathers. Brief and to the point, it summarizes well each stage of child development. It covers the salient points a father needs to be aware of and tells simply how to handle his child and his role as father."

Dr. Padama Talcherkar spent 30 years in private practice of Pediatrics. She practiced at hospitals including Cook County Hospital and University of Chicago Wyler Children's Hospital. She taught Pediatrics at Rush University Medical School and Southern Illinois University Medical School.

Introduction

"I'm going to be a what?"

You get the big news. You're going to be a father. That goofy look passes over your face. You're trying to look happy, while fear and doubt wrestle within your brain. Your mouth gets dry, your stomach flips. Your bank account seems to shrink. The mobility and self-indulgence you share with your spouse will soon be gone. Your mate will become more interested in someone else. Your life is about to change forever. You're thrust from boy to dad in the short period of nine months.

We are men. We are not inclined to ask for directions. We are the hunter-gatherers, male explorers of a world we regard as our dominion. We are expected to be experts at the world's most important job. Fatherhood. Most men are not prepared. There are no classes to teach us how to be good dads. We either go by intuition or imitation, or try to do the opposite of our fathers.

"New Dad Handbook" shows a new father what to expect and

offers some tips, tools and tricks on how to handle himself and his child. It explores the ten stages of a child's life from newborn through 18 and beyond. It's about good humor, good habits, good talking and good listening. It's a lot of work. And a lot of fun.

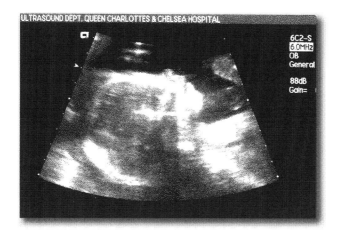

1

you're going to be a Dad

You a dad? You're having enough trouble, just being responsible for yourself. Now you're going to have to be responsible for a kid for the next 20 some years and more. Is this the end of your softball team? Should you sell your golf clubs? Is it the end of poker nights with the boys? These and other nagging questions kept you awake at night. Doubt, fear and dread wrestled in your head. You passed from panic to excitement, through terror and resignation. Worst case scenarios played in your head in the middle of the night. Your spouse's body transformed. She went through fear, morning sickness, indigestion, glowing, budding, bulging and bitching. You were to blame. You just stood by dumbly waiting. What was a couple, is now to be a trio. Or perhaps even more! Congratulations, dad.

Your mate got all the attention. People surrendered their chairs. Friends and family gave her showers and gifts. You were relegated to the background. Where you belong. You acquired a lot of new stuff that didn't belong to you. Clothes, toys, furniture, wheeled carts, car seats, slings, backpacks, bags for carrying things that are not yours. Diapers, wet wipes, baby clothes, blankets, toys, gadgets, pacifiers, baby food, etc. - all the excess baggage you will carry with you everywhere for the next several years - all for your new baby.

Your companion swelled into extreme discomfort, kicked from the inside, imbalanced by her protruding stomach, robbed of sleep, deprived of mobility and stretched and transformed into something entirely beyond herself. She lost her wardrobe. She lost her sex drive. She lost patience with you. Her emotions ran through her like changing scenes in a fast paced TV commercial. She cried easier. She angered faster. She wanted to eat strange things at all hours of the day and night. You had a hand in this too. Or to be more accurate, some other part of your anatomy. She carried the burden, sacrificed her body and suffered the aches and pains. You just moped along, feeling sorry for her and yourself. And in the end, she went through indignity, excruciating pain and exhaustion. And through it all you stood by dumbly, watching and waiting. In the delivery process, as she pushed, they pushed you out of the way. And suddenly, there it was. The long anticipated and promised miracle. Your baby. Now it's time to step up and take your place. As a dad.

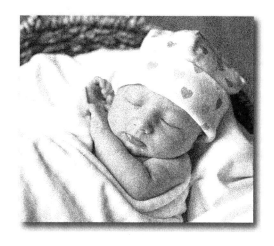

2

Hi Dad

Congratulations on your new baby, dad. It's an amazing feeling. Now you know the paradigm shift. Wow. Now you understand. Are you getting used to the changes? Time has new meaning. Space has shrunk. Home is cramped, crammed with all kinds of new stuff. You are no longer a boy. You are officially an adult. You are now in possession of someone you care about more than yourself. Here lies a helpless, wondrous part of you and your mate. Something miraculous has transpired. Your focus has shifted from yourself. You will dote on, worry about and champion the causes of this little life, beyond your own. Forever. This is your immortality. Someone beyond your potential. Someone who will, in the natural order, live beyond you. Your job is to make sure not to screw it up. To help, not hinder. To encourage, not discourage. To nurture, guide and teach, all in the right directions. Here is someone to keep healthy, fed, clothed and clean 24/7 for the foreseeable future. To worry about for the rest of your life. Welcome to fatherhood. Are you ready?

The nest has been prepared. Your baby has a bed, clothes and all that other stuff you've accumulated. It's time to put all it to use. Your mate arrived home frightened, relieved, excited, exhausted, hungry and slightly sick to her stomach with worry. The nurses are gone. The experts have abandoned her at home. You are now the support system. The baby is asleep in the crib and when it wakes, the two of you are expected to be mom and dad. What next?

Most of it will come naturally. Your mate wants to hold and caress, cuddle and coo. She will also be exhausted and need some help. You may be afraid to hold your baby. You might fear breaking it, or doing something wrong. You might want to avoid contact as long as possible. Don't. Babies are pound-for-pound, less breakable than you. Support that oversized head and cradle it in your big strong arms. The baby will like this and you will too. As prune faced and misshapen as most newborns are, this one may look to you the most beautiful baby you have ever seen. It may have your big nose or sleepy eyes or silly ears. But, it's yours. It wants you as much as you want it. It's time to get to know each other. Savor this amazing process. As you will say later, it's all too brief a time in your lives.

You've heard of post-partum depression? Not everybody gets it. It's a fancy name for fear, fatigue, hormonal changes and the overwhelming realization that mothers suddenly have a lifelong dependent. She is allowed these feelings. Acknowledging them will help you both get through it and on to the joys of discovery. Encourage her to admit her fears. Get some help. A mother, an experienced relative or friend can help take some of the pressure. She needs to get her strength back. If negative feelings persist, take her to a pro. The burden is not all hers. She needs rest and sleep and her own solitude. She will recover faster. You can help. Encourage your mate to eat well, stretch, breathe deep and listen to music. Give her some rest. Learn to change diapers and feed if you're equipped. She can't pour a lot out of a glass until it's filled.

Remember, you have not lost your mate, you have gained a child. One of the rules of nature is "Babies 1st." You will not be the center of her attention for the near future. Be prepared to understand that her hormones are adjusting, thus affecting her moods. She is exhausted. She feels ugly and misshapen. She has no sex drive. Be understanding. Pitch in and help, or find someone who can. A kind word or gesture goes a long way. Learn patience, Dad. Don't be the other new baby in the family.

8

WARNING

Oh yes, and start the baby's college fund now.

CHECKLIST

☐ Help your mate. Be a good sport and back-up. You're a team.

☐ Get your hands on and your arms around your baby. You will both benefit from it.

☐ Remember, you rank third for the near future.

?

∫+age 1 – neʍborn +o ? mon+h∫

Your baby will sleep most of the time, for the near future. There will be brief interludes of eating, pooping and peeing, but sleeping and growing are its main activities. Babies should sleep on alternating sides, their back supported by a rolled blanket. Not on their backs or stomachs, or with blankets, pillows or stuffed animals nearby, because their necks aren't sufficiently developed to move their heads away from breathing impediments. And for the same reasons, infants should NEVER sleep in the same bed with mom and dad. As much as this seems natural, it is extremely dangerous. If Mom is nursing, you can help by bringing the baby to her and returning it to it's bed after feeding. Keep it in your room, if you feel more secure, but you will hear it, even down the hall. You understand the concept. Just help as much as you can.

Wash your hands before and after handling baby. You may have been grocery shopping and pushing the cart, shaking hands, petting the dog or handling a phone. Who knows where unwanted germs gather. Get into the hand washing habit.

Crying is alarming to new parents. Newborns generally cry for three reasons. They're hungry, tired or wet. Sometimes they just want to be held. Sleep will be the most natural state for the next several weeks. Birth was an exhausting experience for your baby too. What's going on is the process of development and growth. Watch the eyes twitch, the mouth smile or pucker in imaginary nursing. Stretching feels good after being cramped inside mom all those months.

As a dad, you need to learn how to handle changing, feeding and burping. It's good for Dads and babies too. When your baby wakes, feed it first. When it's nearly full, change the diaper. If it poops, you may want to change if first, but it's up to you. You'll get into your own rhythm, depending on your speed and skill. Sometimes they are ravenous and really need to eat to relax and make changing easy. Breast-feeding. Obviously, you will be of little use here. But, you can be helpful. Fetching baby, changing and bringing it to mom will be appreciated. If you're using formula, you can do it. Feeding gets a little air into baby's stomach. After a few ounces they will begin to squirm. Pulling up knees and grunting are other signs of gas. This means burp time. Hold baby upright over your shoulder, supporting the head with one hand, gently patting or rubbing the back with the other. After the burp, it's back for more. Always end feeding on a burp to avoid spit-ups.

Changing is about cleaning. The options are mild soap and water and packaged throwaway moist wipes. The important thing is how you wipe away poop. Grip the baby's ankles and lift. Start with the big load first, then dab away the details. For girls, always wipe away from the vagina. Pay attention to all the cracks and crevasses. Newly circumcised boys, will have a gauze pad protecting the tender end. Clean gently and reapply a fresh dressing. If boys are uncircumcised, clean under the foreskin. Wrap up the waste and dispose of later, after you've redressed and put the baby down safely.

As baby rests, so can mom. Sleep cycles usually go for three to four hours but can vary. It's no fun to be awakened in the middle of the night, night after night. That's where a good dad can be helpful. If mom needs a night off, pitch in. Well-rested moms reward good dads in wonderful ways.

The cycle of sleep, eat, change will continue for many weeks. There will be increasing times of waking for your baby. They love to be talked to and sung to. Your voice is familiar. It has been hearing mom and you too inside for many months. Soft caresses and easy massages feel good, just as they do for you. Watch as your baby discovers the world. When holding, support the head until it's able to hold it up. At this point, baby's heads are far more developed and heavier by proportion than the rest of their bodies. They taste, smell, see and hear. Music is good for the mood. Think of it as a sound track for your life. At this stage, you can make a lot of noise without disturbing a baby's sleep. It's time for you and your mate to devote some time to each other.

The baby is rested, fed and changed, but it's still crying. Why? Check for fever, clothing pokes, pinches or obvious signs of discomfort. OK? What is it? Obviously, babies can't communicate, so parents have to surmise the trouble. Are we always cheerful, cute and cuddly? No. Sometimes babies are what you could call fussy. Most likely it's gas. A little gentle back rub or pat, or rocking will relieve the pressure. Holding them on your lap, stomach down can be a comfort too. The warmth of your body against theirs can bring gas out. Swaddling is comforting. Wrap the baby snugly in a light blanket. It's like being cradled in the womb. Maybe the concept of boredom enters the picture. After all, sleeping, eating, pooping and peeing can get tedious. So, a little talking or walking might help. Show them colors. Put on music. Talk to them. Often a pacifier will help. Some babies just like to suck. Crying can be exercise. It's a natural part of a baby's development. Lungs expand, voices sound. It is distressing to parents. It should not last long. Your ears will become tuned to the casual cry, in contrast to the distressed cry. Pain sounds different from fussy. Some babies suffer a bout of colic. Stomach aches. We don't know why. When in doubt, call the pediatrician.

Newborns are extremely portable. It's time to get out into the world. Mom has been cooped up for all these months. Pack up the baby and all that other stuff and go. Get a good fitting car seat that faces the rear and buckle in the baby comfortably tight. Put baby in the back seat. It's the safest place for car travel. Babies rest easily in car seats at restaurants. Grandparents and relatives love visits by the new star of the show. Here is your chance to show off and brag a little. Your mobility is limited and will not last forever. Use it while you can.

No baths until after the umbilical cord falls off (1-4 weeks.) For the first year, bathe two or three times a week. Too much bathing dries their skin. If you can wash a car, you can bathe a baby. Pay attention under necks and in all the cracks and crevasses. Try to keep water out of ears, as they are prone to blockage and infections. Mom will teach you. Babies like baths.

HERE'S WHAT TO PACK IN BABY'S TRAVEL BAG. Diapers, wipes, tissues, cotton balls, carry sing, bibs, small blanket, sun hat, socks, extra clothes, pajamas, pacifiers, water, formula or spare frozen breast milk, food, spoon, baggie of Cheerios (or other non-sugar finger food for older babies) small toys, sun block, big plastic bags for dirty diapers (use the free ones from the grocery store and tie the handles to seal) safety pins, band aids, a tube of diaper rash ointment and a small bottle of anti-bacterial hand cleaner. Obviously, get the biggest bag you can carry. Who knew that one this little could have so much stuff to carry?

Being a dad is the most important thing you can be in your life. The more you know, the more you do, the greater the reward. Mom needs your help. She's still recovering, exhausted and learning too. The time you spend now with your baby will be a down payment on your relationship in the future. They enjoy seeing and exploring too. Babies love being held and talked to. The more the better. Pass on the important things you'll need the baby to learn. They won't remember the specifics, but it's good practice for later. Know that babies feel, hear, smell and taste. And yours will know you sooner through all these senses. It only gets better, the older they get.

CHECKLIST - newborn to 3 months

☐ Discuss an immunization schedule with your pediatrician.

☐ Baby sleeps on its side, never stomach or back.

☐ Clear bed of toys, loose blankets, other breathing impediments.

☐ Baby is NOT to sleep with you for obvious reasons.

☐ Wash hands.

☐ Learn to feed, change diapers and clothes and burp.

☐ Pitch in for middle-of-the-night duty.

☐ Don't forget the diaper bag.

☐ Enjoy getting to know your baby.

4

Stage 2 – 3 to 6 months

This is what you've been waiting for. Your baby knows you. Even looks like you in parts. Smiles and giggles are your greatest reward. Personality is blooming. Dimples are dimpling. Cute is the word. You are highly entertaining. Your silly faces are appreciated and emulated. Your voice is recognized. Your appreciative audience is assured. Babies recognize other babies. People are noticing your baby. The world is revealing itself. It's fun to watch.

Babies babble, blow bubbles and find their hands and feet extremely fascinating. The mouth is the depository of all things foreign. Cereal and other new foods are stimulating to developing palettes. Messes are easily made and part of the fun of exploring. Creeping on the floor is the prelude to crawling. Put down a clean blanket. You've been walking in the outside world. Clear the decks for curious explorers. Here is the stage where objects within reach are moved beyond the perimeter.

The baby should be sleeping through the night. If not, it will soon. For most new parents, not soon enough. We not only teach our children, they teach us. In this case patience. And how to function on little sleep. Get them on a schedule. This is really important and will serve you throughout their lives. The schedule is something you and they can rely on. Make a schedule that fits your lifestyle. If you're a late-nighter, keep them up later. They'll sleep later in the morning. They will accommodate you. Longer sleep cycles are usually triggered by the introduction of cereal. Cereal is more filling and babies sleep longer.

WARNING

Don't fatten your baby for your own convenience. The tendency is to over-feed. Don't make food a reward or distraction. Heed the warnings about overweight kids becoming overweight adults.

If your mate is nursing, weaning can happen in this period. Your pediatrician will be your guide. Waiting too long can make weaning more difficult. Emerging teeth can be motivating for moms. Mom's breasts become tender, swollen and sore in the weaning process. Dads can't be of much use here. Just be patient and realize that the breasts belong to mom and the baby for the time being. Later in this cycle babies get into varieties of fruits, vegetables and meats. Finger foods are introduced. Baby has established taste favorites. Since teeth are yet to be of service, stick with gum food.

Using sign language works at this stage. Say "more" using a simple hand sign, to see if they want more to eat. "Finished" is another sign. You can make them up, or use American Sign Language gestures. Babies can communicate through signs before they can talk.

Emerging teeth can be cause for sore gums. They can get cranky, runny noses or swollen gums. Soft chewy toys help. Try keeping one in the freezer to sooth tender gums. Ice chips are fun too. They are a plaything as well as a cool treat. If pacifiers are a part of the scene, keep plenty of spares. There's nothing worse than groping in the dark in the middle of the night, searching for a dirty pacifier.

Your baby is extremely agreeable and portable. Give mom an occasional break by taking the little one with you. You'll be a hero.

Take mom out for a date. At this stage any friendly relative or sitter is a happy experience for the baby. Leave contact and emergency numbers written down for the sitter. Help mom resist the temptation to call every half hour from the party, restaurant or movie theater. A regular respite is recommended for everyone's sake. If you haven't already noticed, your prospects for romance have returned. Make the most of it.

CHECKLIST - ? TO 6 MONTHS

☐ Talk to, hold, play with, communicate with your baby. They absorb more than you know. Start now and keep it up forever.

☐ Get baby on a regular schedule. It will help you later.

☐ Use sign language for simple concepts. Baby will too.

☐ Give Mom a break. Take your baby out with you. Show it off. You'll get so many compliments for being a great dad.

5

stage 3 – 6 to 12 months

Big mobility changes here. Crawling, pulling up on furniture and eventually walking. This means everything within baby's reach has moved up and beyond. Lower the mattress in the crib to accommodate your little stand-up comedian. With mobility comes the ability to explore and satisfy curiosity. Babies love to poke fingers in holes, electrical outlets and animal's orifices. Curiosity leads them into, under and atop places they often shouldn't be. They are mobile trouble seekers. This is that 24/7 cycle you've heard so much about. Adult eyes must never leave babies in this stage. Sharp edged furniture is shoved out of the way. Cabinet handles are secured with strong rubber bands. Electric plugs are filled with plastic guards. Pet food containers are removed from temptation.

By now your child has lots of toys, but would much rather play with pots, pans and spoons. Let them. Maybe they will love cooking some day and you will be the beneficiary of some fine meals. Large empty cardboard boxes are fun too. There is nothing like an empty space to crawl in to satisfy curiosity. Play with other kids is good too. It's a fine opportunity to spread germs, get into toy tugging matches and poke into each other's noses. It's all part of building a strong immunity system. Washing hands is always a good thing, before and after.

There is some controversy about infants watching TV. The educational stuff is good for entertainment and learning. Obviously, pro wrestling, explosions and shoot-outs aren't what we want them to imprint. A playpen and a good kid DVD is an effective short-term babysitter for a busy parent. Be your own judge. Go ahead when you need to give something else your full attention.

Babies love hanging with dads. Take them with you. Mom gets a break and you get to be a hero to both of them. Baby's personality is imprinting. You are an important influence, even at this early stage. Do the feedings and baths. Read together. Play on the floor. Be the playground. Help with the bedtime routine. Have fun being a kid too.

Time for a new car seat for the little one? Look for one that grows along with your baby. You'll need one, or at least a booster, until your child reaches 49." There are some remarkable car seat/stroller combos out there. They can be expensive. Consider a resale shop. Car toys are good to carry. Favorite stuffed animals are quiet companions. For pacifier babies, linking one to the car seat is a safeguard against loss. Long car trips are as unpleasant for babies as they are for us. When fussiness peaks, it's time for a rest stop.

In this stage bedtime routines are established. Kids like a regular routine. A bath or wash, a bedtime storybook and a quiet goodnight in bed with the door closed, all begun early and on schedule, will pay off in the future. Kids who tell their parents when and how they want to go to bed rule the roost. Do you want to be a leader or follower?

WArRning

Keep the baby out of your bed. That's your place. A Saturday or Sunday morning romp is OK, but don't let them sleep with you. You will suffer for it later and so will the baby. Babies have their own time and place for bed and like it that way, if you do it right.

CHECKLIST – 6 to 12 months

☐ Lower the mattress to accommodate your stand-up comedian.

☐ Move sharp edge furniture out of the way.

☐ Secure cabinet handles with rubber bands, fill electric plugs with plastic guards.

☐ Take "Dad Trips."

☐ Feed and bathe. Give Mom a break.

☐ Read together at bedtime on a schedule.

☐ Get down on the floor and have fun.

6

ʃtage 4 – 1 year to 2

This is a big year. Walking, talking and balking. They are fast and mobile. They can ask for things. They understand you. They know when you are telling them not to do something, and testing you to see if they can get away with it anyway. The squatty, cherubic look gets longer and leaner. They have outgrown their baby clothes. They have favorite hats, toys, stuffed animals and other inanimate objects. They are possessive and selfish. They want mom's full time attention. Or dad's. They can become wary of strangers, or even casual acquaintances. This is all natural.

They do not want to share with friends or siblings. They can hit, pinch and bite. The best way to handle this is to call attention to the evidence of their behavior. "Look how sad he feels when you won't share your ball." "You hurt her. Look at the red mark where you pinched." Or. "No biting. It's dangerous and bad." They understand at this stage, but often will continue to react physically. Building empathy is good and important for later. Separation is a punishment. It stops everyone's fun.

21

Seeing toddlers discover the world is a joy. Books are a wonder. Read to them. Read to them. Read to them. I will encourage this over and over and over. Kids will magically be drawn to books later in life and, as a result, be better students. I promise.

Art is a stimulating imaginative outlet and should be encouraged early. It's great for manual dexterity and creative development. Crayons, chalk and paints are a fascinating mess. The kitchen table is a handy place that's easily cleaned. They don't always understand that paper is the medium of choice for these new toys. Don't be surprised if your budding artist suddenly decorates your walls and furniture. Keep an eye on them and encourage their art. Save the good stuff. Grandparents love it.

Music is fun and good exercise. Dancing will reveal creative moves you've never seen before. Dance with them, it's good for you too. Teach them songs and sing together. Got an instrument? Let them play with it. Developing a love for music will be a joy to them forever. Kids who study music do better in math and languages. Fact.

They love to go places. They will be happy to help you shop. Keep them strapped in the shopping cart for their safety and your sanity. Have friends and their kids over. Being with other kids of varying ages teaches them valuable social skills and how to deal with inevitable conflicts. Your internal tendency will be to always take your child's side. Be fair and honest. Deal with your own first. If another kid commits a foul, separate yours. They will get your meaning, and other parents won't be bent out of shape. The less said, the better.

Toys are great, but imagination is better. Let them find amusement in themselves. You'll buy an expensive toy and they'll play with the box it came in. Good. Their imagination is bigger than the toy. Build a tent out of two chairs and a blanket. Couch pillows are fun pile-up toys. Empty paper grocery bags are filled with magic. Big boxes are playhouses. Magazines have lots of pictures. Pots and pans are exciting. Open closets are fun to explore. A little solitude is a good thing. You don't need to be the entertainer. Being dad is a big enough job.

If a second language is spoken in the house, use both. Young minds are sponges for information and language. Show them things and name them. Colors, objects, animals. Ask them questions. Speak softly, they will speak softly. Speak loudly, they will do the same. They are constantly watching and listening to you and others. They understand more than they say. Even at this age, you will be surprised what they might blurt out in front of grandma. The more you talk to them, the better they will talk.

Toddler-proofing the home is fairly simple. What they can reach, on their tiptoes or by climbing on furniture, is fair game. Don't get ridiculous and move everything up above the tide line. Just the dangerous stuff. Glassware, sharp trinkets, small swallowable objects, anything you don't want to disappear. You can make them understand that certain things are off limits. A quick verbal reminder when they reach for something they shouldn't is enough of a deterrent. After a while, they will read your look, testing you with an approach to something they know they shouldn't. Toddlers are much smarter than we realize.

Potty training. They don't like diapers any more than you do. They get the concept. Try reading time on the potty. It combines a favorite pastime with something new and interesting. When the deed is done, excitement and praise are great rewards. Pride will draw them to repeat this positive experience. Don't rush it, but give it a try. They might see how you or mom do it and suggest it themselves.

Tooth brushing chores have been yours. It's time to start positive habits for them. Let your child use the toothbrush. Praise efforts and do a finish up. Electric toothbrushes are best and come in attractive kid pleasing shapes. Encourage them to put the top on the toothpaste and put everything away. When it becomes a ritual, it's easy. It's all part of the bedtime routine.

Learning is fast and furious in this year. The more you show them, stimulate them and challenge them, the greater the response. They remember everything. They forget selectively. The world is opening fast to fertile minds. Take them places. Show them things. Watch them learn. Toddlers crave anything new. It's time for joyous overnights at grandma and grandpa's. It's time for a break for you and mom.

This is the time you've been waiting for, Dad. You have a pal. He or she will follow you anywhere. They will try anything. Roll a ball on the floor. Get some puppets. Draw together. Read. Show them the things you're interested in. Take mom out for breaks. Or be the babysitter and give her some time to herself. She will love this. Yes, she will love you for this.

WARNING

Small children of any age should never be shaken, jiggled or tossed in the air. It may look like fun to you, but it can be harmful to necks and brains.

CHECKLIST – 1 year to 2

☐ Build empathy. When your child hurts another, call attention to other's feelings.

☐ Separation is punishment. Hitting and yelling aren't allowed.

☐ Read to your child. Read. Read.

☐ The arts are fun. Art, music playing, listening, singing, dancing.

☐ Take them places. Show them things.

☐ And empty box can be more fun than an expensive toy.

☐ If you speak a foreign language, speak it to your child.

☐ Warn them of dangers.

☐ Make potty training fun by reading, praising.

☐ Get a sitter and take Mom out.

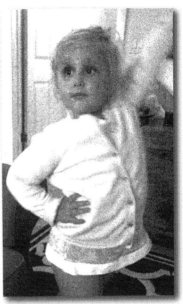

7

stage 5 – terrible 2s and 3s

You've heard of this dreaded stage. What makes two so terrible? Your toddler is talking, fully mobile, discovering the world and has likes, dislikes and desires. What you want doesn't count. It's full speed ahead, after anything of interest, be it dangerous or fascinating. The mindset is, "I'm curious, I'm able, I have my own mind. Why can't I do what I want?" It is one of the biggest challenges to a parent. How can you let discovery progress, without causing harm or damage? Good luck.

Here are some basics for handling the terrible toddler. One of your best tools is distraction. He or she wants something forbidden. A saltshaker. Introduce something else of interest. A spoon. This doesn't always work. Nothing does. A firm explanation that, "This is salt. It can make you sick." is enough of a reason. Give another choice that you define. Rather than your toddler playing with your phone, offer a favorite toy. "This is mine and it's not a toy for kids. Let's play with your "whatever." Good luck again.

Don't negotiate! If "don't" doesn't work, redirect. It they reach for a knife, say "Thank you. That's very dangerous. Let's put it away." If they test you by frequently approaching the pet's bowl, take it from them and say, "Thank you. That is yucky and belongs to the dog." Redirection is a good way to change bad behaviors, by reinforcing the idea of their making a good choice. Simple logic is tough to verbalize to an inner directed toddler, whose mind set is, "Me want this." Good luck here too.

The temper tantrum. We've all seen them. The child seizes control of the situation, screaming or collapsing on the ground while the exasperated and embarrassed parent tries to deal with it. Temper is frustration. They want something they can't have. This problem has roots in behavior at home. If it works, kids will push until they get what they want. Don't compete in the game at the child's level. Be above it. Don't be drawn into bad behavior. Don't offer bribes or deals. Walk away. They are looking for a reaction. Tantrums don't work if you ignore them. Define limits early and set consequences. Follow up and don't back down. Always be firm and resolved. Explain what you expect. Kids like to please, if you handle them right. Suggest ways for kids to get what they want within reason. Amazingly, even little ones are capable of reason. Happy kids know what they can and cannot get away with.

Punishment. We know that adults can injure children physically and psychologically. I don't advocate hitting our yelling. A lot of older folks talk about the good old days when spanking was a deterrent to bad behavior. Physical reactions in anger are destructive. A gentle touch with a sound attracts attention. It means, "Stop and pay attention to me, I don't approve." It should be followed by a quick explanation of the infraction. Separation is a good punishment for repeat offenders. Some call it "time out." Giving them time alone stops the aberrant behavior and changes the environment. It gives everyone time to cool off. Nobody has the perfect solution to these problems. Full-grown adults still have problems with behavior. The roots start in childhood. It's important to remember that kids are like your five fingers, they're all different. The same punishment applied to one will have a different effect on another. Never compare one child's behavior to another. Never degrade. Better to lose a privilege than to impose a consequence that frightens or is in any way harmful. No matter the age, punishment should be brief and fair. Never scary. Scaring can be scarring.

It's important to establish that both parents are on the same page. You are a united front, not a good cop, bad cop. Get together on dos and don'ts. Don't let you child negotiate one against the other. Don't negotiate in front of your child.

"It's time." Here is a magic phrase that is a cause for action. "It's bath time." "Bed time." "It's time to get dressed." "It's time to eat." Toddlers get used to schedules. When it's time, get up and go. Don't use it as a warning. Act now. They will appreciate the conditioning and be aware that schedules are for organized lives. The Rolling Stones were right. Time is on your side. Yes it is.

Kids live in the present. Past and future mean little. Realize that what is going on now is where their attention lies. Distractions from an unpleasant now can turn into a more pleasant now. Don't threaten with some future consequence. Kids don't get that. "If you don't do (whatever) now, you won't get (whatever) in the future." doesn't work. Make it simple. Make it now.

Choices. Give them only two. More than two is confusing. Milk or juice? Sweatshirt or jacket? Peanut butter or cheese? Make both choices good for you.

Here's a tip for a pacifier dependent child who won't surrender. Tie the pacifier on a short string to a doorknob. When the child needs a fix, the prize will be there, hanging on the door. Boredom and embarrassment will eventually lead the child away.

Two through three is a wondrous time, full of exploration and wonder. The brain is soaking things up faster than ever and wants to know and experience everything. Read, talk together, play music, sing, speak other languages, open doors, take trips, meet people, communicate feelings, build rich and varied lives. This makes for better adults.

If pre-school is an option, take it. The earlier the school experience, the better, both academically and socially. Early students make better student.

Everything done together now is fun. Team up for the dog's bath. It can be a fun, lasting memory. Whatever you've dreamed for them starts now. Play musical instruments together. Great piano joy starts here. Let them look through the digital camera and take a few shots. It won't cost you a thing. Get miniature sporting goods. Try the resale shops, as they will soon outgrow everything. Go to little league games in the neighborhood together. Look for junior golf clubs. Tiger Woods started at two. Resist the temptation to live out your own fantasies, but help them find their own.

CHECKLIST – Terrible 2s and 3s

☐ If your toddler wants something forbidden, distract, explain, substitute.

☐ Don't negotiate. Be the dad. Redirect.

☐ Ignore temper tantrums. Don't give in. When they cool, suggest ways they can get what they want.

☐ No hitting. No yelling. Explain any infraction. Separation is punishment. Time-outs cool things off, you too. No matter the age, punishment should be brief and fair. Never scaring. No degrading. No comparing one child to another.

☐ Be on the same page as Mom. Present a united front.

☐ A Magic Phrase – "It's time." For bed, bath, time dictates action now.

☐ Kids live in the present. Don't threaten. It doesn't work.

☐ If pre-school is an option, do it.

☐ Play together. They'll learn so much from you.

8

stage 6 – 4 to 6 years

This is magic time. Young minds are inquisitive. They can communicate fully. They analyze and speculate. They see the world from a new and unique perspective. They know phonies. They are completely honest. They don't know how cute they are yet. This is my favorite time. They are open and capable of teaching adults a thing or two. They can learn to read, if they've been read to. The can sing and play music. They have developed physical dexterity. Talents emerge. Foreign languages are readily absorbed. Physically and mentally, they are capable of almost anything new. They form interests. They see possibilities. They make connections.

They are verbalizing their impressions of the world, unfiltered, unedited and with complete candor. They haven't learned political correctness, thankfully. Words of wisdom often emerge when truths are realized. Their observations can be hysterically funny. Get out the pen and paper and save these verbal gems for grandparents and posterity.

Early pre-school and early reading make for better students later. Everything begun in this period gets a head start. This is golden time.

They have thoughts and feelings, preferences, likes and dislikes. Reason takes a larger role in their thought process. They are watching and listening to you. You can expect to see your behavior played back. Early positive routines are good habits now.

A word about praise. Give it when it's deserved. Not just for showing up. One of today's tragedies is giving trophies for wearing a uniform. Trophies go to the best.

The long-term goal. You are building an adult. Your job is not to make a copy of yourself; it's to make something better, something beyond your greatest potential. In this time of dawning realization, you have the opportunity to spark the light of reason, independence and logic. To build compassion, insight and understanding. This generation is our hope for the future. Our legacy. You have the amazing gift of a child, born with an A+, and have the responsibility to do all you can to keep from diminishing that promise.

If you thought the last stage was good, this is better. Real talents, skills and abilities emerge here. Take them to a professional ballgame, or kid play. Take an afternoon at a museum or antique car display. Take them to swimming lessons, now while water is fun and nothing to fear. Have them hold the flashlight while you try to figure out what's causing a drip under the sink, before you screw it up and call the plumber. Let them scrub the tires when you wash the car. Memorable hose fights start here. Let them help you rake leaves into a pile and jump in. Make creative sandwiches together, like peanut butter and raisins. Create together. Read together, letting them do the reading. Include them in all you can. Show them the way. You will both be rewarded for the experience.

Gender awareness. "Boys will be boys" doesn't carry the same meaning it once did. Some boys like toy guns and cars, some like cooking utensils and dolls. The reverse is true with girls. Don't push, don't bend. They are breakable. Let them be who they are.

CHECKLIST – 4 to 6 years

- ☐ Teach them. The arts, sports, activities, languages, etc.

- ☐ Pre-school. Yes.

- ☐ They are who they will be. Maximize their potential.

- ☐ Expose them to the world.

- ☐ Let them help. Work and play together. Show them the way.

- ☐ Have them read to you now.

9

STAGE 7 – 7 TO 10 YEARS

These are the confidence building years. Time to choose activities, develop talents, and pursue interests. Get music lessons. Get into art. Get into theater or dance. Join a sport, club or activity. Learn to cook. Take responsibilities. Show them how to make their beds. Let them help prepare meals. Have them put away laundry. Give them a plant to nourish. Care for a pet. Understand the difference between following and leading. Let them feel the rewards of their independent accomplishments. Help them grow, learn and have fun.

Again, stay close and keep talking to your kids. If you see something special in them, tell them about it. Show them. Help them develop that quality. Show them other sides of the city, country and world. Travel. Help them understand other points of view. Analyze other's behavior and talk about it. Make your feelings known and ask about theirs. Ask them questions about things for which you don't have answers. Challenge their imagination.

Stay in touch with teachers. Help organize and monitor homework. Know their friends. Have their friends to your house and make them welcome.

Don't let them win easily at games you play together. They may expect to win easily in more important games later in life. Encourage them. Show game strategy and help them work to improve skills. Try chess.

Teach "The Golden Rule." Treat others as you would have them treat you. Make them understand "bullying" and encourage them to come to you if it happens. Give them tools to deal with the situation. Show them the basics of manners, etiquette, compromise and ethics. Teach a firm handshake and a look in the eyes. Show compassion for the less fortunate, the aged, animals and all living things. Do good things for others for no reward, other than the joy of giving. Teach them to listen carefully and thoughtfully to others, even those with which they may disagree. Encourage them to reasonably speak their minds. Teach them to manage money. Let them transact minor purchases. Save for the future. Get them a piggy bank. Give to charity.

Thank you notes. It's time for them to express their gratitude for gifts given. Show them how and why it's important. A habit started now will be an admired trait later in life.

Let them have fun and explore. Trust them for the good judgment you have taught. Allow them creativity in their music and fashion while discouraging fashion slavery. Make them aware of advertising and marketing and how they influence wants as opposed to needs. Ask what they feel about these influences.

Celebrate family traditions. These are fun and bonding events children look forward to. Make some new ones of your own.

Feed them well and often. Encourage sun block. Recycle. Discourage needless waste. Encourage their sense of humor. Enjoy them.

Go to their games, plays, and recitals. They need your approval and support. Don't embarrass them by being loud, just be there. Don't heap praise where it is not warranted. Express your unconditional pride, whether they succeed or fail. Encourage them to try again. Take them to work with you. Find a neighbor who needs help, maybe an older person who could use a hand mowing the lawn and bring your child along to help. Buy your child books. Better yet, take them to the library and get their own library card. Let them browse. Make suggestions. Show your child how tools work. Help build their confidence by showing them how to do their best. Encourage their natural idealism. Ask them questions. Ask their opinions. Ask for their help. Keep the lines of communication open.

WARNING

In our culture, we can't let our kids roam free. So, we risk over-organization, over-protection, and over-supervision. Don't press them into every sport, activity and opportunity. In short, don't over-parent. Don't cheerlead. Don't push. Don't think you have to entertain. Let them fill their own free time. Quiet solitude has value. Imagination grows where activity slows.

CHECKLIST – 7 to 10 years

☐ Help develop their confidence, choose activities, pursue interests and talents.

☐ Teach the difference between leading and following.

☐ Give them responsibilities. Make bed, help prepare meals, put away laundry, care for a plant or pet.

☐ Travel with them.

☐ Help them understand point of view and behavior. Ask their opinions. Challenge their imagination.

☐ Know their friends and teachers. Help with homework.

☐ Don't let them win at games easily. But, encourage them.

☐ Teach the Golden Rule, manners, etiquette, compromise and

ethics.

☐ Show compassion. Do for others. Encourage sharing and charity.

☐ Encourage them to listen well and speak their mind.

☐ Let them make small purchases and handle money.

☐ Celebrate family traditions. Start new ones.

☐ Teach them to recycle.

☐ Get them a library card.

☐ Listen to and talk to them. Be there for them.

10

STAGE 8 – 11 TO 13 YEARS

Teach them about of alcohol, drugs and cigarettes. It you abuse any of them, you lose your credibility. They will be most influenced by your behavior. Alcohol is accepted in moderation in adults. They want to be adults. Make them understand the damage that can be done by excess. Avoid lectures. A good technique is to tell a story about someone. A true-life account will be a more memorable lesson than all the platitudes you can pronounce. Sadly, everyone knows of an alcoholic, lung cancer victim or drug addiction tragedy. Make them understand peer pressure and how to diffuse it. Help them develop leadership skills.

Talk about family, local and world history. Analyze the mistakes of the past. Encourage their natural idealism. Ask them to visualize how the world should be and how people should be treated. Encourage exploration in academics, sports and activities. Make opportunities for discussion on any subject open and nonjudgmental, even if you have to bite your tongue. Ask open questions. Listen to them. Talk less.

Allow them free time, privacy and solitude. Teach them to appreciate silence and inactivity. The attraction of video games, the computer and TV are strong. They needn't be denied. But, when things get overboard, try a road trip to a quiet place. Bring apples and enjoy the sights and sounds of nature. A half hour in your enjoyment of silence might be therapeutic to your child as well. They might even initiate conversation on their own. These can be golden moments.

This is a tough time in a child's life. Huge changes are taking place in mind and body. It can be a difficult time of self-doubt and insecurity. Discuss body changes and sex with humor and understanding. Moms should talk with daughters about the body changes associated with menstruation. And what's happening to boys. Dads should explain what's happening to boys at this age too. And what's happening to girls. Explain the dangers of unprotected sex. Sexually transmitted diseases are rampant. Emphasize that unprotected sex can lead to disease and pregnancy. Make sure your daughter knows that HER BODY IS HER OWN. Teach your boys respect for the woman's point of view in a world of male dominance. Use books to help you. Knowledge helps eliminate fear and anxiety, building self-confidence.

I knew a family with 12 children. When one of the kids came home, Mom always smiled, hugged and greeted them by name. When dad came home, he made it a point to speak with all his children individually. This seemed the most gracious way parents could make their child feel important. Try it. Watch their happy faces light up at your attention and affection.

Assign them responsibilities around the house and set consequences for failure to satisfy them. Be firm but flexible. Expectations are better than rules. Be the adult.

I can't stress enough how important it is to try to maintain closeness and contact with your kids at this stage. They will want to pull away. Give them slack, but stay with them. They really need you.

This is the start of the tough times. Pre-teens have fertile minds.

What is planted there will grow readily. If you remember your own youth, kids will want to separate themselves from parents at this stage. It is normal. Give them the leash, but hold the end lightly. Keep talking and use your sense of humor. It is your best resource.

CHECKLIST – 11 to 13 years

☐ Teach them about alcohol, drugs and cigarettes and how to deal with peer pressure. You are the best example.

☐ Talk about world events, history. Ask them to visualize how the world should be. Encourage their natural idealism.

☐ Listen more. Talk less.

☐ Take them to nature.

☐ Discuss self-doubts, body changes in both genders, sex. Stress the importance of protected sex and the dangers of sexually transmitted disease.

☐ Show them you love and respect them.

☐ Give them responsibilities and set consequences for failure to satisfy them. Expectations are better than rules.

☐ Maintain closeness, but give them slack. But, keep talking and keep your sense of humor.

||

STAGE 9 – 14 TO 18 YEARS

Here come the Terrible Teens. Were you the perfect teenage son? How much of what you did were your parents aware? Remember? You didn't like your parent's music, clothes, politics or hairstyles. You spoke a different language. You wanted to express your individuality. You wanted to be what we called cool. You wanted to be accepted by your group. You wanted to spend minimal time at home. Getting it?

Today there is even more competition for your teenager's attention. Social media, TV, cell phones, computer games. The Internet connects them with the world. Cell phones bring them friends, photos, email and instant messages. The world is available instantly. Teenagers already know a lot more about a lot more things than you do. So, why do they need you anymore? It's your job to show them. They still have a lot to learn. So do you.

Family meals. Yes, it's nearly impossible to juggle everyone's schedule to eat together, but it's one of the most important times for communication and bonding. Eat together. Talk. Ask questions.

Show affection. Just because they're grown up, they still need a hug, kiss, or kind pat. It's this kind of unspoken communication that keeps everyone together. Monkeys groom each other for the same reasons. Be monkey-like.

Help make sure they get enough sleep. We know that teenagers need more sleep than the rest of us. Most schools start too early. Help them get to bed early enough. Easier said than done.

Stay in touch with their friends. They are the mirrors of your teen. Continue to encourage them to bring friends home. This is the last place they want to be. But, you need to be encouraging anyway. Food is always a big draw, especially among insatiable growing boys. Know where they are and where they're going. Know when to expect them home. Establish limits, but be reasonable and flexible. Again, expectations are better than rules.

Be familiar with their high school curriculum and make sure it's relevant to their planned college experience. Meet with school guidance counselors about college choices. Ask your child to participate in a college expense budget with you. Get them a checking account and maintain the balance monthly. Encourage them to get a part time job in the summer for their own spending money. Teach them the courtesy of writing thank you notes. Teach them job interviewing skills.

Help them recognize they were born with gifts – their talents and traits that come easy and fun. If they do it well and love it, they will be good at it. Encourage their talents. Someone smart once said that talents are gifts to you. And that your responsibility for your gift is to develop your talents. Encourage them to get advice, serve apprenticeships and seek internships with pros. Allow them to chase their dreams. Youth is the time to experiment, to seek out the new and exciting. There are thousands of ways to make a living. Their goal should be to enjoy making a living. Not just to get rich and be famous.

Teach them the basics of car care. The importance of regular oil changes, fluid level checks, brake wear and tire pressure. In their early teens take them to an empty shopping center parking lot and show them how to drive. Let them park between the lines and get the feel of a car for acceleration and braking. Practice often, well before driver's license time. They will be more accomplished drivers when the time comes. Show them the expenses involved in car maintenance. Insurance, fuel and other upkeep. Have them take charge of helping keep the car clean. Make them familiar with the expenses of running the home. Groceries, utilities, insurance, rent or mortgage. Make independent living something they understand to reduce surprises later.

Ask them to plan and cook a meal. Give them kitchen clean up and dish duty. Show them how to do their own laundry and ironing. Take them shopping for groceries and have them keep a running mental tab of the total. Put them in charge of younger siblings for an evening. Have them call their grandparents once in a while.

Keep in mind that the high school years are the years of rebellion. It just isn't cool to be with parents. Did you want to hang with your folks? By this time, the teenager has pretty much made up his or her mind that they know just about everything there is to know about what is truly important to them. I always called this the "young lion syndrome." "I am grown, tough and smart and I don't need you." It's a perfectly normal and false assumption. After all, they are on their way out of the nest. As college departure time approaches we often see the "leaving nest anomaly." Young adults pick fights with parents. Parents react by pushing back. It's what birds do when the young take flight. It's a simple mechanism for assuring that the trauma of separation is softened by a tough exterior display. This too shall pass. They will be back.

What's the most important lesson here? You're building on all your efforts to this point. You can only hope that by your example and exposure, you have built a responsible, thoughtful leader. He or she will be tested by peers, tempted by the culture and tried by unseen circumstances. You have a teammate on your side, your mate. Stick together and back each other up. Be a dad, not a best friend. Your job is to keep communication open. Listen more than you talk. Remember your sense of humor. Get through the bad stuff and enjoy the good stuff. Now they are old enough to share interests and even teach you some valuable things.

CHECKLIST – 14 TO 18 years

☐ Remember what it was like to be a teenager.

☐ Keep communicating. Know what's going on. Good luck.

☐ They think they know it all, but still have a lot to learn. Stay as close as you can.

☐ Show affection. Yes, it can be difficult, but do it.

☐ Eat together. Yes, it can be difficult, but do it.

☐ Know their friends. Encourage them to your house.

☐ Let them know of your expectations, but be flexible.

☐ Be familiar with their high school curriculum and get to know their guidance counselor. Important for college planning.

☐ Encourage them to follow their talents and gifts.

☐ Teach them to drive early and practice a lot. Teach them the basics of car care and maintenance.

☐ Get them a checking account or prepaid debit card and teach them how to use it.

☐ Encourage summer jobs for spending money, deposited into their bank account.

☐ Give them duties around the house. The lawn, the garage, some cooking, laundry, babysitting and shopping chores. They'll gripe, but thank you later.

☐ Be the dad, not the best buddy. Be firm but fair. You and Mom are a team, be consistent and on the same page.

☐ When they're ready, let them go. If you haven't done it right by now, it's too late anyway.

12

STAGE 10
THE REST OF YOUR CHILD'S LIFE

And so, as quickly as they came into your lives, they are already departing. Two things happen at this time. Parents either fall into depression or celebrate their new-found independence and mobility. Perhaps a little of both. Young men and women off to college also make an amazing transformation. In hindsight, most parents don't look so archaic and dumb after all. Indeed, as the years progress, parents seem to get smarter.

Are your worries over? Of course not. These days, after college we often see our children return for another dose of lodging, food and shelter from the big world out there. Parents will always be parents and children always children, far into old age, when the roles often reverse.

If you follow the advice in this little book, at least you can rest assured that you have prepared them as best you could, given your level of sensitivity, patience and energy. You will make mistakes. So did your parents. So will your children. But, at least you will have each other. And the great comfort of caring and love.

Well, the kid is gone. But not far and not forever, if all goes well. Let's hope you heeded my advice in the first stage of your child's development and started the college fund early. Now it's time for you and your mate to enjoy your time together. Work on that relationship for a while. There are places to go, things to see and lots to learn. Enjoy it all together. After all, the kids will be back. And maybe with kids of their own. Then the real fun starts. You get to be a grandpa.

RECOMMENDED WEBSITES

www.kidshealth.org A comprehensive website dedicated to children's health and well-being, established by the Nemours Foundation. It covers General Health, Emotions & Behavior, Growth & Development, Nutrition & Fitness, Pregnancy & Newborns, Medical Problems, Positive Parenting, First Aid & Safety and Doctors & Hospitals.

www.circleofparents.org A network of parent-led self-help groups where parents and caregivers can share ideas, celebrate successes and address the challenges surrounding parenting.

www.newdadhandbook.com See our recommendations for great kid products and services.

ABOUT THE AUTHOR

Robert Richter is a multi-award-winning writer, director, composer and artist. He's written short stories, memoir, commercials, novels, screenplays, songs and children's books. He's directed hundreds of commercials for major advertisers and their ad agencies. His music plays in films, documentaries and commercials. His art decorates walls, greeting cards and children's books.

"Weekend Away" and "In Defiance of Gravity" are his novels.

"Stairway to Heaven" "Vegas Weekend" and "Last Night in Paris" are volumes in The Gold Collection – Outstanding Short Stories. "Bedtime Stories" is a compilation of all 95 of his short stories.

"The Line" won the Gold Award for Children's Picture Books, Mom's Choice Awards.

"Bill the Bird" is for kids and celebrates physical diversity.

Collect all his books, available at amazon.com, Kindle, iBooks, or his website www.rrichter.com.

19492092R00033

Made in the USA
Middletown, DE
05 December 2018